6TH GRADE HISTORY: FIRST CIVILIZATIONS

BABY PROFESSOR
EDUCATION KIDS

The cradle of civilization is a term referring to locations where civilization is understood to have emerged independently.

ANCIENT MESOPOTAMIA

Teheran
Namak Lake
Asadabad Pass
(7241)
11073
Diyala
Dez
Qom
P E R
P E R
Isfahan
Zard Kuh
14921
14100
Karkheh
Q
M
I A
Karun
Euphrates
Hawr al Hammar
Basra
Shatt al Arab
ahra' al Hijarah
Bubiya
12

Mesopotamia is considered to be the cradle of civilization. It was here that people first gathered in large cities, learned to write, and created governments.

The most important
advance made by
the Mesopotamians
was the invention
of writing by the
Sumerians. They
wrote on tablets
and drew pictures
which represented
ideas or objects.

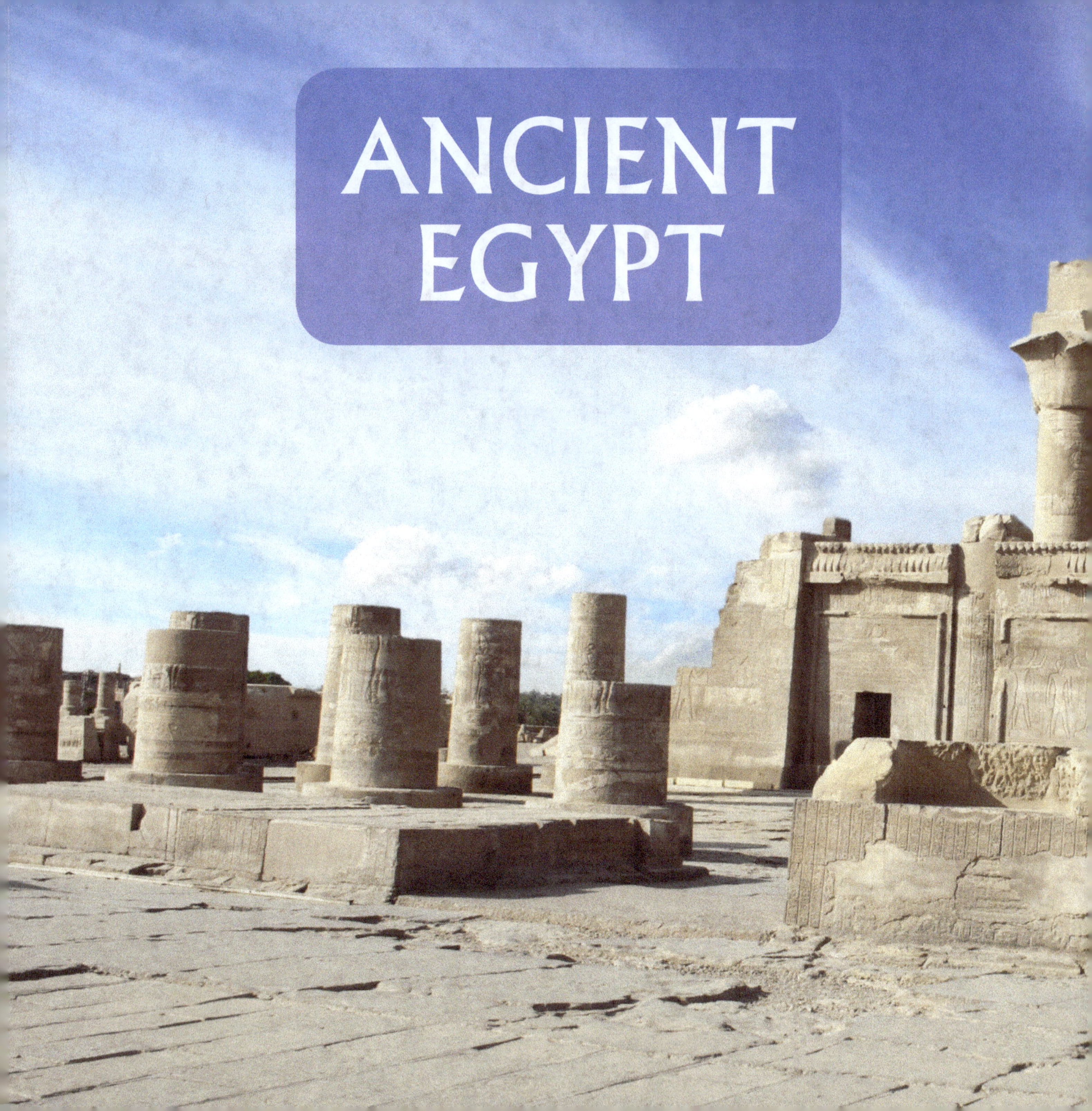

ANCIENT
EGYPT

Ancient Egypt was one of the greatest and most powerful civilizations in the history. The civilization of Ancient Egypt was located along the Nile River in northeast Africa.

Ancient Egypt
was rich in
culture including
government,
religion, arts,
and writing.
Some of ancient
Egypt's crowning
achievements,
the Giza pyramids
and Great Sphinx.

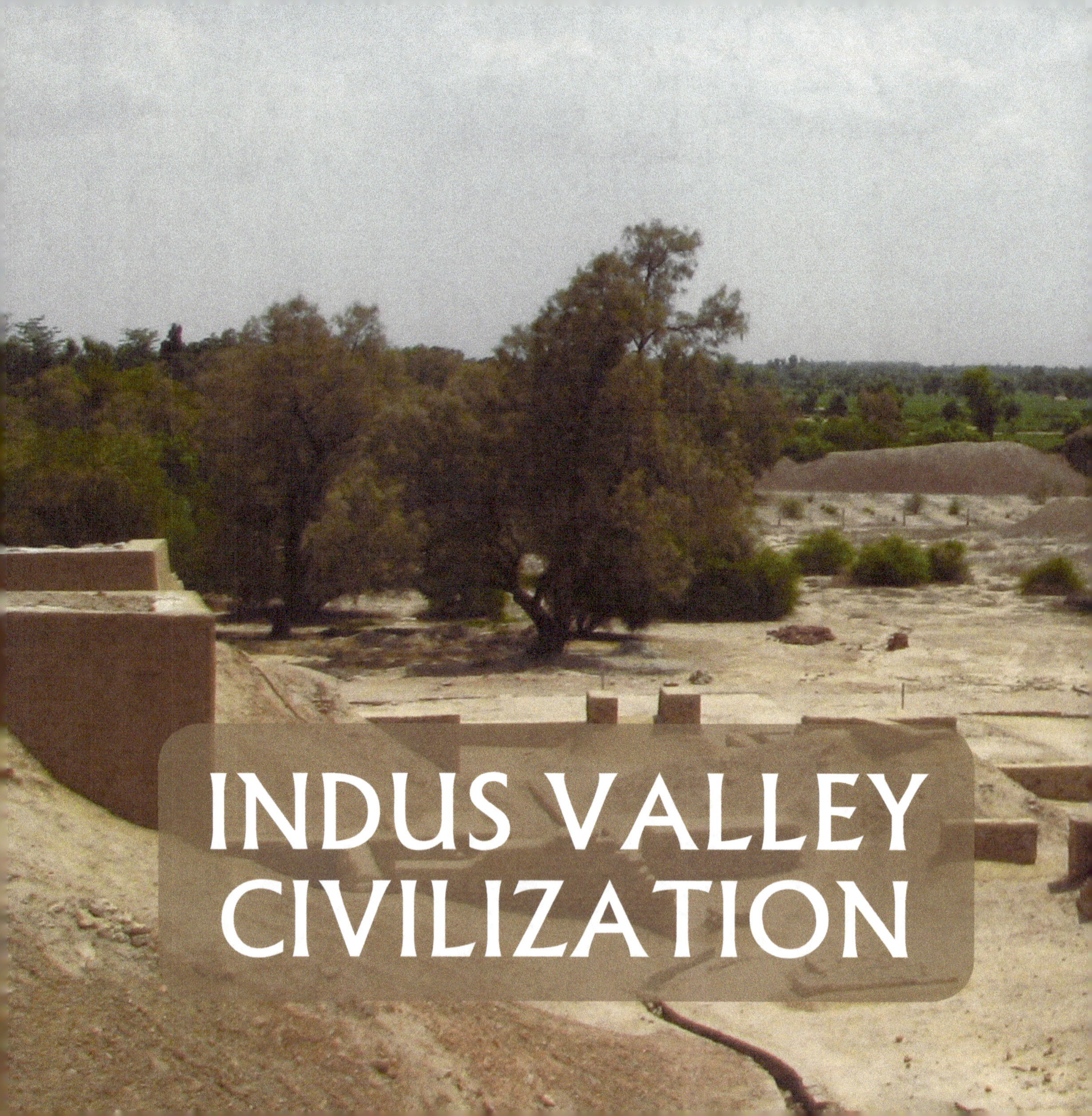

INDUS VALLEY
CIVILIZATION

Origin of the Indus Valley Civilization lies between 3300 – 1300 BCE. the Indus Valley Civilization geographically extended to Egypt or Mesopotamia.

Indus Valley Civilization was flourished in the basins of the Indus River, one of the major rivers of Asia. The Indus Valley Civilization had a total population of over five million.